Life Lessons from Proverbs

Jack Nordgren

Practical applications for life from the book of Proverbs

Cover photo by Jason Sutton of Paul Gregory (aka Moose aka Ziggy) headed out to catch some waves in St Joseph Michigan

ISBN-13: 978-1500252434

ISBN-10: 1500252433

Dedication

This book is dedicated to my three sons:

Jason Wesley Nordgren

Joshua Robert Nordgren

Josiah David Nordgren

Proverbs 23:15-25
My son, if your heart is wise, then my heart will be glad; my innermost being will rejoice when your lips speak what is right. Do not let your heart envy sinners, but always be zealous for the fear of the LORD. There is surely a future hope for you, and your hope will not be cut off. Listen, my son, and be wise and keep your heart on the right path. Do not join those who drink too much wine or gorge themselves on meat, for drunkards and gluttons become poor, and drowsiness clothes them in rags. Listen to your father, who gave you life, and do not despise your mother when she is old. Buy truth and do not sell it: get wisdom, discipline and understanding. The father of a righteous man has great joy; he who has a wise son delights in him. May your father and mother be glad: may she who gave you birth rejoice!

Forward

After my Dad died, I was given his Living Bible. Right inside the front cover, he wrote down every year that he read the entire Bible through. By 2003 he had read his Bible through 27 times.

The translation he read was the Living Bible. It was first published in 1971. The Living Bible is a paraphrase of the American Standard Version of the Bible. The author, Ken Taylor, translated it after he started paraphrasing the King James Bible for his children. He was trying to put the Bible in modern day language for them. His goal was to make it easy to understand.

My Dad read a chapter from Proverbs every day. Often he would quote a verse from Proverbs that applied to a specific person or situation. Many times he didn't quote Proverbs. He would just live it in front of me.

I found a book marker in his Bible that my sister gave him. The words printed on it sum up my sentiments as I write this book.

Dad
I'm thankful for the knowledge you've given me...
for your faith in God which serves as the example
by which I live...

For your patience and understanding which helped me look beyond myself. For all these things and more, I'm so thankful you're my Father!

On the back of that marker is the verse:

"The glory of children is their fathers."
Proverbs 17:6

Then she writes:

Dad, Thanks for wanting one more child but most of all for living God's Love, I love you so much!
-Annette

He also underlined two verses:

My son, how I will rejoice if you become a man of common sense. Yes, my heart will thrill to your thoughtful wise words.
Proverbs 23:15-16

My Dad wrote my name next to those verses. It is my prayer that this book will be just that: *"thoughtful, wise words."*

Table of Contents

Chapter 1

A Longing Fulfilled

Proverbs 13:19a *"A longing fulfilled is sweet to the soul."*

I'll never forget it. It is as clear in my mind as if it just happened yesterday. I was just watching TV when all of a sudden every siren in the city went off! The sound was deafening. People were running out of their houses screaming at the top of their lungs! They were jumping and hugging and some were even crying.

It wasn't the end of World War II. The year was 1959, and the Chicago White Sox had just won the American League Championship. Having been raised on the south side of Chicago, my Dad and I were die-hard Sox fans. Our two favorite teams were the White Sox and whoever was playing against the Cubs. I still have the whole 1959 White Sox line up memorized.

Fast forward to 2005. I am living in Hawaii and I get a call from my sister, Annette, to get home as soon as possible. My father is ill. He might not make it.

This same scenario had happened to my Dad 10 years earlier. In 1995, I was in a pastor's meeting in Honolulu. I got the call about 1p.m., and by 4:30p.m. I was on a plane headed to Chicago. Dad and Mom had moved to Michigan, so after the 8-hour flight I had 1 ½ hour drive to the hospital. As I entered the hospital room, I hugged my Mom and two sisters, Annette and Arlene. Dad looked up and saw me and said, "Am I that bad?"

I stayed for a week. My older sister, Arlene had been a huge help, making sure Dad got the care he needed. He got better. After that, I thought Dad was invincible. In my mind he was too tough to die. He had been drafted into the Navy in World War II. His ship was a decoy for the Kamikaze planes. The fatality rate on those ships was one in seven, but he survived.

He went on to survive several colon cancer surgeries. But the cancer came back. Now, here we were in 2005 and Dad was too old and too tired to go through another surgery. After spending time in the hospital he was put in Jordan's Nursing Home under Hospice care.

Every day we would all visit and spend time with Dad. At the same time, it just so happened, our beloved White Sox were in the World Series. So every night after getting home from the hospital, I would stay up and watch the game. I saw every single one, but I did fall asleep during Game 3, which lasted 14 innings.

On my last day before flying back, I stopped to see my Dad one more time. I knew this would probably be the last time I would see him on this earth. I was sad but I was also excited. I had some good news that we had been waiting for, for a long time.

I told him, "Dad the White Sox won the World Series last night."

He responded, "You're kidding."

"No, they really did."

All our lives, we had been rooting for our Chicago White Sox. Year after year, we were longing for the coveted title, "Winner of the World Series," but we were disappointed. Now, after 88 years for my Dad, and 58 years for me, they finally won the World Series. Yes, we were "longing" for many years, but that's why it was sooooooo "sweet to the soul."

That moment was one special memory I will forever treasure in my heart. I feel like it was a special memory that God in His infinite wisdom wanted to give to my Dad and I.

I miss my Dad a ton, but I believe with all my heart I will see him again. My Dad's Living Bible has this following scripture underlined, *"Let not your heart be troubled. You are trusting in God, now trust in me. There are many homes up there where my Father lives, and I am going to prepare them for your coming."* John 14:1-2.

The "Longing Fulfilled" I experienced the day I told my Dad that the White Sox won the World Series is going to pale in comparison to the day I knock on my Dad's front door in Heaven and say, "Hey Dad…I'm home!"

Chapter 2

Hope Deferred

Proverbs 13:12 *"Hope deferred makes the heart sick, but a longing fulfilled is sweet to the soul."*

Maybe I watched too many Disney movies growing up. I thought that when I got married my wife and I would live happily ever after. I thought it would just happen. After years of marriage, it didn't. My hope was deferred. My heart was sick.

It was my Father who said, "Marriage isn't for sissies." He was right. I found out the hard way it takes a lot of work.

I felt like I had fallen into a black hole and there was no way out. Things between my wife and I had never been worse. We were not communicating. We were not close physically, emotionally or spiritually. I was into porn, which gave me brief moments of satisfaction, but only helped temporarily. It wasn't a lasting fix. In fact, after the momentary euphoria, I just fell further into the black hole of depression.

There were a number of stressful things going on at the same time. First, my mother-in-law was living with us.

Over the years, she had always been such a help with our kids, and boy, could she COOK! She was from down South.

Now in her nineties, not only was her sight deteriorating, but so was her mind. She had dementia and was constantly doing irrational things. One night, while sound asleep, I awoke to the dog barking, the phone ringing, and someone knocking at the door. My dear mother-in-law had wandered out the back door. She wasn't that far from the house but she was lost. After that we had to secure the doors so she couldn't get out. On top of this, my wife was babysitting our grandkids 20-plus hours a week. Normally this wouldn't be a problem, but with the mother- in- law situation, it was overwhelming.

In my mind, I was going over my options. The pain was so bad; I even entertained suicide. At least it would end my pain. Then I thought of the emotional wreckage that it would rain down upon my family, my friends, and our church. That thought stopped me dead in my tracks. No, that wasn't the answer. How about divorce? That would be hard on the family. What would that say to my three sons? When the going gets tough, just bail out. My father always taught me that a man is only as good as his word. I had always tried to be a man of my word. I made promises on our wedding day so that option was out. I could just grit it out and let things continue on like they were, but that was too painful. Or, I could pray and try to talk things out with my wife. My hope of a great marriage had been deferred and I needed to do something. I was dying on the inside.

The last option seemed to be the only one that offered a glimmer of hope. After praying, I came up with a word picture. I wrote it out. It was the story of an old pair of shoes. In the story I told her that I felt like I was the old pair of shoes. I was comfortable to wear but there were new shoes that had become more important. The old shoes were not very important anymore. I was scared to death to share it with her but I did. I remembered what my Dad had said: "Marriage isn't for sissies. It takes a lot of work." I took the chance of being rejected.

SHE HEARD ME! I was so glad because now we were going to work on this together. We went to see a marriage counselor. This lady was awesome. Both my wife and I had emotional baggage from our past that was weighing us down. She helped us to see it and deal with it. We had a lot to talk about. Certain things that my wife would say and do would trigger some deep seated rejection issues in me that I hadn't dealt with. My wife had lost her Daddy at a young age. She was afraid to love me deeply, because she might lose me too.

Things didn't get better overnight. We had a lot of work to do. We started making changes. We started going out on dates once a week. Sometimes these dates were in the middle of the day. It was the only time that would work with our busy schedules. We talked ALOT. On days we didn't have the grandkids, our good friend Jim would come over and keep my mother-in-law company while my wife and I went to the movies.

Once a week, I would walk my mother-in-law over to my son's house for a couple of hours so we could have a romantic evening and sexual intimacy. It was a longing fulfilled and it was sweet to the soul. I now had the great marriage I had hoped for.

It wasn't easy. It took a lot of work. It took prayer. It took a Spirit- filled counselor. It took time. Was it worth it? My wife and I have been married for 44 years, and THINGS HAVE NEVER BEEN BETTER. I am more in love with her than ever. We are close emotionally, physically and spiritually.

People may tell you that if you're married for a long time, sex will get boring. That's true if you are growing farther and farther apart, but if you're growing closer to God and each other, it just gets better. I wouldn't trade my wife for any other woman in the whole world.

SHE IS DA BESTEST!

I regularly tell her, "Of all the women in the world, you're just the right one for me."

If you are married please remember: “MARRIAGE ISN’T FOR SISSIES. IT TAKES A LOT OF WORK”. Right now you may feel like you have, “hope deferred that makes your heart sick”. No matter what happens don’t ever give up. Keep working at it. Keep praying. Keep hoping. Don’t settle for anything but that “longing fulfilled (because) it is sweet to the soul.”

Chapter 3

Living at Peace with Your Enemies

Proverbs 16:7 *"When a man's ways are pleasing to the Lord, He makes even his enemies live at peace with him."*

Over the years I have written a list of names next to this verse. Let me tell you about the first one. One day, our 10-year-old son came crashing through the front door of our mobile home and exclaimed,

"Troy Bettis says he's going to beat me up!"

Even though Troy was a year younger than our son, he was a head taller. Troy had a reputation for being the biggest and toughest kid in the neighborhood. Nobody messed with him.

We had just moved into a trailer park in St. Paul, Minnesota from Hawaii so I could attend Bethel College. Moving had been quite an adjustment. After getting so used to the local people and culture in Hawaii; this adjustment was quite challenging. Hawaii has its own language (Hawaiian & pidgin English), customs, food, and music. It’s the only state that is a chain of islands. In Hawaii, our boys stood out like a sore thumb. When picking them up from school, it was quite easy to spot them. They were the only two white-skinned towheads (blonde hair) streaming out of the building after school. All the other kids were of Asian/Pacific Islander descent and had brown skin or black hair.

Now, in Minnesota, it was hard to pick them out. We haoles (Caucasians) all look alike! Our boys were just one of the many towheads. The first day picking them up from school I actually had a moment of panic trying to find them in the crowd.

After the move, things seemed to be going along pretty well. Our two boys, Jason and Joshua, seemed to be making a few friends. Then Troy Bettis happened. As parents, we were beside ourselves. We didn’t know what to do.

I sat down with my son and we talked about it. Neither of us had an answer. I wanted to go talk with Troy. Jason wouldn’t let me. He said that would only make things worse. We talked and talked, but we couldn’t agree on a plan. Totally at my wits end, I said to Jason, “Lets pray”. As we prayed, I felt the Holy Spirit tell me to take Troy to McDonalds.

After we finished praying, I told Jason. He freaked out! He felt for sure Troy would just beat him up at McDonalds, but I was sure of what the Spirit had told me to do.

I took the boys over to Troy's house and asked his mom if we could take him to McDonalds. Troy's mom, a single parent, said yes. She was elated that someone was taking an interest in her son. We took Troy to McDonalds and had a great time. It became apparent that nobody had ever done anything like this for Troy. On that day, he and Jason became best friends.

Back at the trailer park, things changed for our boys because Troy was now watching out for them. Nobody messed with the Nordgren boys because if they did they would have to answer to Troy. As a result of all this we even invited Troy to go to church with us. Eventually Troy's mom came too.

It was after this incident as I was reading Proverbs, that the Lord directed me to write Troy's name next to this verse. I understood that it was the LORD who had caused our enemy to live at peace with us. It is my prayer that all who read this book will begin their list too.

I have a list of names in my Bible next to this verse. Troy's name is the first of a long list.

Over the years I have come up with 3 rules for my enemies:

1. Pray for them
2. Look for an opportunity to do good to them
3. Tell them about Jesus

Luke 6:27-28: *"But I tell you who hear me: Love your enemies, do good to those who hate you, bless those who curse you, pray for those who mistreat you."*

Romans 12:17-21: *"Do not repay anyone evil for evil. Be careful to do what is right in the eyes of everybody. If it is possible as far as it depends on you, live at peace with everyone. Do not take revenge, my friends, but leave room for God's wrath, for it is written: "It is mine to avenge; I will repay," says the Lord. "On the contrary;*

If your enemy is hungry, feed him; if he is thirsty, give him something to drink. In doing this you will heap burning coals on his head. Do not be overcome by evil, but overcome evil with good."

You may ask the question: "Does this always work?" The answer is, "No". Sometimes it doesn't...but my batting average is way over .500!

An interesting postscript to this story:

When my son Jason's daughter, Bethany, was in the third grade, she got unwittingly involved in an incident at school. One of the girls in her class had threatened another via a handwritten note. Bethany had seen the note and who wrote it. The teacher found out about it and asked the class who wrote the note. Bethany told the teacher who the author was, and was now the target of some bullying from this girl and her friends at school, who had landed in some major trouble because of it.

Bethany came home incredibly upset about the situation and the bullying she was now encountering. My son Jason and his wife Rachel weren't sure what to do…but then Jason remembered a trailer park in St. Paul, a boy named Troy, and a trip to McDonalds.

Jason and Rachel called the school principal and told them of a grand scheme to bring the girls back together as friends. The principal was aware of the problem with the girls and was all ears for a solution. They asked to have the parents contact information, and invited all the girls over to their house on Friday night for a fun get together.

That Friday night, the parents dropped off the girls at their home. Teenage girls from Jason and Rachel's youth group were on hand to give the third-grade girls a complete spa night: makeovers, hairstyles, manicures, and pedicures! They hosted snacks for the girls and they all had a wonderful time.

By the end of the night, the girls were all friends again. Appreciative parents picked up kids who were not fighting with each other anymore. Bethany had no more trouble from any bullying at school. And my son passed a life lesson from Proverbs that he had learned to his children.

Chapter 4

One Hundred Blows

Proverbs 17:10 (NASB) *"A rebuke goes deeper into one who has understanding than a hundred blows into a fool."*

I stood there stunned, speechless. I couldn't believe what I had just heard. I felt like I had just been hit in the head 100 times. I walked away in silence. I had gone to the back of the hardware store to tell my sister that she was spending too much time on the phone. After I did, she let me have it! I felt like I had just been buried by a 50-foot wave at Waimea Bay.

When I rebuked her she responded, "Oh yeah, well Erik told Dad that he busts his a** waiting on customers, while you corner someone and witness to them".

I was a new Christian. Even though I had been raised in church, I really didn't know what it was to have a relationship with God. I had taken my own route and at the ripe old age of 23, I found myself on a dead end street. God had delivered me from a lifestyle that was killing me. I was excited and I wanted to share it with the world but I had no idea that I was coming off as a jerk to my fellow co-worker.

Erik Hamlin (who liked to be called “H”) had been raised in the same church as me. He had gotten into the party scene. He was a great worker and a good hardware man. He knew his stuff. Even though he had diabetes he still wasn’t deterred from the lifestyle I had just left behind.

I was pretty subdued the rest of the day. The next day I was praying and reading my Bible in the morning and I came across this verse. I knew I had to change. I asked God to help me.

The hardware store had a new employee that next day, and his name was Jack Nordgren. God changed me. The first thing I did was to thank my sister for telling me. After that I was a much better worker. If I had the opportunity to share my faith with someone, I would keep it brief and ask them to meet me later rather than cornering them down some aisle for an extended time.

I left the hardware store about 5 years later to go into the ministry. When I left, I wasn’t sure if my change in behavior had any effect on “H”. About 20 years after my sister rebuked me in the back of that hardware store I received a letter. As I read the letter I sobbed. It was from “H”. He was now married and had two children. The diabetes and his old lifestyle had taken a toll but he had become a different person. He had not only had a relationship with Jesus, he was an elder at his church. In the letter he thanked me for my Christian witness. He told me that I had been a great example for him.

“H” never knew what my sister said to me that day. He never knew how it had hurt me or how much it helped me. My sister’s rebuke went deep and hurt more than a hundred blows. It hurt my pride. It went deep because it was true and the Holy Spirit was convicting me of my pride and showing me my need to change. It’s the one time I’m glad someone took the time to let me have it.

Chapter 5

A Word Aptly Spoken

Proverbs 25:11 *"A word aptly spoken is like apples of gold in settings of silver."*

I was driving down Diamond Head Road in Hawaii on my way to a funeral. It would turn out to be the most unusual funeral I would ever officiate. This funeral was for a drug dealer that I had never met. On top of that, I had just found out that my friend who asked me to do the funeral didn't tell anyone that I was coming. I was scared. What if they all got angry? In my mind I could read the headlines in the Honolulu Star Bulletin: "PASTOR KILLED AT DRUG DEALER'S FUNERAL."

I remembered hearing on the news a few days before about a murder in Waikiki. A young man was stabbed and it took several hours for him to bleed out. It was a slow agonizing death. I also remember thinking that it must've been drug related.

Now, here I was on the way to do his funeral. What the heck was I going to say? I didn't have a clue but I knew that this was a great opportunity to share the greatest news in the world. I shot up a quick prayer. I needed the right words to say.

I hadn't been a stranger to drugs. Back in the 60's my friends and I got pretty involved. It got bad and I was in deep. I needed to find some help and I got it. What I found wasn't religion, but a relationship with Jesus Christ. He changed my life and now I had an opportunity to share it.

A couple musicians from our church shared some songs. I remember them playing "Stairway to Heaven" by Led Zeppelin. The people loved it. Then many of the people started taking turns sharing about their departed friend. After everyone was done sharing, his ex-wife said stood up and said, "What do we do now?"

The Holy Spirit spoke to my heart and said, "You're up!"

My friend who invited me stood up and said, "I invited Pastor Jack to come here and say a few words."

Two gals from our church, Dee-Dee and Afton, had told me they had shared with the now-deceased dealer about Jesus, and how He died on the cross for his sins. Remembering this, I really wasn't sure what I was going to say, but as I stood up, the words started coming out.

I started by sharing my hope that their dead friend had remembered what had been shared with him by Dee-Dee and Afton, and that I hoped he had asked for Jesus to forgive him and come into his life before he died. I spoke some more words that the Holy Spirit gave me in that moment. At the end I thought, "Well, I better see if anyone wants to ask Jesus into their lives. Maybe, just maybe, there will be one or two."

I asked them to pray a prayer with me if that was their desire. To my amazement everyone began to pray. THEY WERE ALL PRAYING IN UNISION! I was stunned! There were about 30 people in all that prayed the sinner's prayer. I totally did not see that coming. We hung out and "talked story" (made small talk) for a while. The funeral ended and we all left.

As I drove home back up Diamond Head Road what had just happened started to sink in. God had just blown my mind. One minute I'm thinking these party people were going to kill me for talking about Jesus, and the next they were giving their hearts to Him. God had given me a word aptly spoken.

I was scared but I had prayed and trusted in God, and He had given me the words to say. I've never had a piece of jewelry that was apples of gold set in silver but I can imagine that it is beautiful...but maybe I don't need it. What God did at that funeral was just as beautiful.

Chapter 6

The Kind of Problems You Want to Have

Proverbs 14:4 *"Where there are no oxen the manger is clean, but from the strength of an ox comes an abundant harvest."*

I was sitting in the back of the hardware store ranting and raving that my coveted delicious Kingsway Vienna Red Hots (famous Chicago hot dogs) were now ice cold. I had been looking forward to this lunch from the time I had gotten up that morning. There is nothing like them in the world. I had just picked up my favorite lunch: one hot dog with relish, onion, pickles and mustard, and a chili dog with onions and mustard. They were wrapped up with the best tasting greasy fries Chicago had to offer.

I still remember it like it was yesterday. Just as I sat down for my first bite, a customer came in. "No big deal", I thought, "I'll just wait on him and then I'll get right back to the delicious dogs". As soon as I finished, I went right back to my favorite lunch. As I was about to sink my teeth into the prize, it happened again. Then it happened again…and again…and again! An hour later I finally got to them. THEY WERE STONE COLD! To say I was disappointed would not even come close to my emotional state.

I know what you're thinking. "Just nuke it!" This was in the early 1970's. Microwaves had not been introduced to the general public yet.

As I sat there in utter dismay, my Dad walked in. He saw my downcast face and heard my mumblings about too many customers.

"What's wrong?" he asked with a wry smile.

I told him my tale of woe. He just smiled and said, "Son, these are the kind of problems you want to have." He went on to tell me about all the times when he had just opened the store when he would sit there for hours waiting for customers to come in.

Years later, I was reminded of my Dad's words. I was at a Pastor's meeting. We were discussing problems at our churches. One pastor needed more chairs. Another had parking problems. And we all had people problems…lots and lots and lots of people problems. You name the problem, and at least one pastor was dealing with it within their congregation: divorce, drugs, alcohol, bad finances, physical abuse, sexual abuse, adultery, etc.

I know many think being a Pastor is easy. I can assure you it's not. We don't just work on Sunday mornings during church. As shepherds, pastors are on call 24/7.

When we as humans come to the Lord, we generally have a lot of "baggage". This baggage is a bunch of real problems that we pick up while following our selfish desires. There is the pain of divorce, the chains of addiction, the weight of financial crisis and a myriad of things that we call in Hawaiian *'hakaka.'* Literally translated, it means "combat" or "fight", but today it can mean whatever brings you trouble.

Now I can assure you that God forgives all sin, but if you rob a bank you will have some *hakaka* in your life and probably do some jail time. When we come to Jesus, there are a lot of messes that come from sin that we need to deal with. The Lord will help, but we still have to deal with the consequences...and pastors are the ones that many people look to for help.

Pastors are great candidates for helping others. Not only have we dealt with our own baggage (and still do); we have a lot of experience in helping others through their personal stories of consequences and reconciliation. It makes sense for pastors to help others wade through their *hakaka*...but sometimes the sheer volume of trouble from other people's lives can be overwhelming.

At the pastor's meeting, many shared that people were coming to faith in Christ by the dozens. Because of this, things were really messy. There were big problems...but these are the kinds of problems pastors WANT to have.

In Bible times, oxen were like tractors on the farm. They helped to get a lot of work done BUT they left a mess in the stable. Someone had to clean up the poop.

During that pastor's meeting, we could have complained about all the trouble. Instead, we were thankful that the Lord was bringing people to Him and lives were being changed. We were thankful for the *hakaka*.

Next time you start to complain about your problems. Ask yourself, are these the kind of problems you want to have.

Chapter 7

Open your Ears

Proverbs 18:13 *"He who answers before listening – that is his folly and his shame."*

In 1978, my family and I moved from Chicago to Honolulu to go on staff with the Waikiki Beach Chaplaincy. It was an evangelistic Christian ministry in Waikiki. They had a Sunday morning church service on Waikiki Beach, a radio program on the top secular rock-and-roll radio station, and a street ministry. Many friends, mentors, pastors, and missionaries gave me some really good advice before we left for Hawaii, but the best advice didn't come from any of them. The absolute very best piece of advice I got came from someone who wasn't a Christian. His name was Skip.

Skip's mother Helen worked for my Dad in his hardware store on the South Side of Chicago. She was a sweetheart and one of the nicest people that God had placed on planet Earth. Her husband was a different story. He was nice enough, but not always dependable. We always knew when he arrived at the store to pick up Helen because of the inevitable earthquake we felt. Well, at least it seemed like an earthquake. He would invariably run his car into the store wall when he parked and shake the whole building.

"Helen, Walter's here."

Good old Walter had been very successful in the shoe business. Somewhere, somehow, booze got the best of him. Eventually, Helen was the only one working.

Now I'm finally getting to the point. They had a son named Skip. He was a giant of a man. He was a kind, considerate, and gentle soul. One day, when I was telling him about the ministry I was being called to in Hawaii, he interrupted me and stopped me cold.

"Jack, I have to tell you something", he said, looking me in the eye. "I'm an atheist and I'm gay".

I was stunned. I had no idea he was going to tell me that. Then he said something I have never forgotten.

"Jack when you get to Hawaii and you open your mouth, open your ears."

I had no idea how important that statement was going to be. I soon found out once I moved to Hawaii. Waikiki has a very large active gay community, and in 1978 it was a subculture woven into the fabric of the city. They had their own beach, nightclubs, neighborhoods, churches, and even their own parade. I, on the other hand, grew up on the South Side of Chicago and had no gay friends. LGBT

(Lesbian/Gay/Bisexual/ Transgender) was not a mainstream term then. Athletes and actors were not "coming out of the closet" on national TV. Where I grew up, being gay was tantamount to having the plague.

Moving to Hawaii was like moving to a different planet. I had no idea what I was getting into, but God did. That's why I believe God gave me this word of wisdom through Skip. Over the years I was able to share the love of Jesus with many people of different lifestyles from mine.

The importance of listening soon became apparent to me. I met many in the gay community through street ministry and prison ministry who just needed someone to listen to them. Over and over, I could hear Skip's words, "When you open your mouth, open your ears." I'm so glad I followed that advice. As I listened, many opened up their personal stories to me. Some of the horrific things that many in the gay community had been through were almost beyond my comprehension.

Let me introduce you to a couple of those stories. One time, an attractive woman began attending one of our evening services. After a few weeks, I noticed that something was different about her. She was dressed like a woman, and she was pretty enough, but she didn't quite look like a woman. It turned out that she was actually a he. She came with a group all dressed as women, and they were all transvestites.

Over the next year we became friends and I heard some of their stories. One that stands out and really broke my heart: as a child, one of them lived with her single Mom. Mom liked military servicemen, of which Hawaii has plenty. Mom would bring them home. But when she left home for work some of them sexually abused him. This happened a number of times. No wonder he was confused about his sexuality and now identified himself as a woman.

These were the kind of stories I would hear. I would feel the love of Jesus as I would listen, hug and cry with them. Jesus had given his life for them.

Let me introduce you to another precious soul that Jesus died for. His name was Wayne. Like Skip, he was a gentle giant and he loved motorcycles. He was one of the best sound techs that Hope Chapel South Shore, the church I pastored in Waikiki, ever had. At one time, Wayne had been part of the gay community.

After contracting AIDS, he became a Christian. He started going to a good church but some things began bothering him. He would hear people telling gay jokes. Then the pastor preached a sermon where he railed against the gay political agenda. He didn't feel accepted and left. Then he found our church, where we were instant family.

He had come to faith in Jesus Christ and left his gay lifestyle, but he still struggled with some of his feelings. He was one of the most open, honest friends I've ever had. Wayne is with the Lord now. I miss him and can't wait to see him again.

During the 1980's, there was a lot of fear and misinformation being spread about gays and AIDS by both the media and by some Christians. A lot of people were scared about contracting AIDS through touch based on their reports. Some churches banned them from attending Sunday services. Instead, they offered to come to their homes for Bible study.

In that time, several from the gay community who had AIDS regularly attended our church. My reaction when I met them or any of their friends for the first time was always the same. First, I would hug them and wrap my arms around them. Then I would "open my ears."

There were many of the LGBT community that came through our doors. Their lives had endured so much tragedy, hurt and suffering, it was hard to comprehend. I did the only thing I knew how to do: love them with the love of Jesus and listen. Then when we had relationship, share Jesus.

Chapter 8

Have No Fear of Sudden Disaster

Proverbs 3:25-26 *"Have no fear of sudden disaster or the ruin that overtakes the wicked, for the LORD will be your confidence and keep your foot from being snared."*

I was riding down H-1 on my motorcycle. As I was thinking about where I was headed, I began to cry. Actually, it was more like uncontrollable sobbing. I don't know how I kept my bike on the road.

I was headed to Kaiser Hospital in Honolulu to see my doctor. I had a pain in my abdomen and had undergone some tests. The results were in, but I didn't know what he was going to say. What could it be? My father had colon cancer so I was terrified that I could die. My Dad's surgery had been successful but what if it was too late for me? What if the cancer had spread too far?

As I was sobbing, I began praying and pouring my heart out to the Lord. I knew Jesus died for my sins and rose from the dead. My faith and trust in Him for my salvation was not in question here. I knew I was forgiven and I would go to be with Him in Heaven when I died. I was just not ready to go. What would happen to my beautiful wife and three sons if I died? What about our church in Waikiki? Who would take over? My mind was reeling with doubts, fears and questions. As I prayed, I felt God's presence quieting my soul.

By the time I saw my Doctor, I had calmed down considerably. The news wasn't good news but it wasn't that bad either. I had diverticulitis. It wasn't colon cancer but it was the stage before. I needed to watch my diet and have regular tests.

It was some time later that I came across this scripture and it jumped right off the page into my heart. I memorized it. Whenever the fear of colon cancer would come into my mind I would quote it out loud to myself.

That was 30 years ago. My diverticulitis has flared up several times since and when it does, I call on my friend. This scripture promise is the friend I call. It is ready to help at a moment's notice. There have been many other "fears" that have tried to assail me. Sometimes they would come out of nowhere and ambush me. When they did, I would call on my friend. Then this verse, like a bodyguard, would jump out in front of me and do hand to hand combat with my fears.

God had brought me and my family through so much already, He didn't want me to let fears buffet me around like strong gusty winds on a motorcycle. Fears can cripple us from enjoying the abundant life that Jesus talked about.

John 10:10 says," *The thief comes only to steal and kill and destroy; I have come that you may have life and have it to the full."*

God wants us to live in the present and enjoy our relationship with Him, our family, our friends, and with His people. Don't let the thief rob you of your joy. Take my friend with you. Take God's promise. The LORD, the creator of the universe is with you. He will be your confidence and keep you from falling into the quicksand of fear.

Chapter 9

Gain More Favor

Proverbs 28:23 *"He who rebukes a man will in the end gain more favor than he who has a flattering tongue."*

I'll never forget the first Sunday that Danny came to Hope Chapel. I had little doubt that he was a musician just by his looks. He had boots laced up to his knees, spiked colored hair, and more earrings in his right ear than I could count.

He was loud and boisterous, but somehow, I just liked him. He was honest about himself and just about everything else. If he didn't like something, it was "bogus". He used the word so much that he came up with a myriad of variations. A person who was bogus was a "Boge". If the person was extra bogus, he was given the title "Bogandi". His name was Danny but it wasn't long before he got stuck with his own nick name, "The Boge".

His good friend, Ike, had invited him to church. The Boge was a bass player. Being a new church, we always needed musicians. It wasn't long before he became a regular and a good friend. As a new Christian, he was hungry to learn more about the Bible. He was like a sponge. Then something happened to change all that: he met a girl. Of course he tried to bring her to church. I say tried because a weird thing happened; every time she came into the chapel where we met, she would get sick to her stomach and have to leave.

Well, it wasn't long before they got engaged. Being their pastor, they came to me and asked if I would do the wedding. We began the premarital counseling. My wife Maree and I do the counseling together, and it didn't take us long to figure out that they were headed for a train wreck. Danny loved the Lord and wanted to serve Him with all his heart; however, his fiancé did not.

I didn't want to tell Danny what I saw coming. He was a close friend and I wanted to keep it that way. Knowing that I had to be honest with him, I asked him to meet me at my office.

I remember it like it was yesterday. I was in my little 6 x 8 office, eating my sandwich. It wasn't just any sandwich, it was my favorite. My wife had made it on her homemade bread. It had sprouts, tomatoes, cheese, turkey and mustard. I was about to sink my teeth into this delicious treat when Danny came in. I offered him the other half. He took it.

As he was eating, I told him that this marriage was headed for disaster. I told him I couldn't perform the ceremony. He went ballistic. He began screaming at me with his mouth full of my sandwich. After I was sprayed with cuss words and various parts of my sandwich, he left.

He went ahead with the wedding. My wife and I attended. I just couldn't bring myself to perform the ceremony but I wanted him to know I was still his friend. It was a tough decision. I wasn't sure how this thing would play out. I just knew I had lost a close friend.

I didn't see or hear much from The Boge for a while. Then six months later, I got a phone call. It was The Boge. He was sobbing.

"She left me," He said.

"Where are you?" I asked.

"I'm downtown on Bishop Street."

"I'm on my way."

As I grabbed my keys I realized it was rush hour. This was going to take a while. I was very familiar with the traffic in Honolulu. I had lived there for over 6 years. Our rush hour didn't even come close to Chicago, where I used to live, but it was bad enough. Miraculously, I made it downtown in 15 minutes. It should've taken 3 times as long.

Danny got into the car crying. He was extremely angry and hurt. He had loved her deeply. I didn't say anything as he poured his heart out. He was broken. I brought him home. He stayed with us for about two weeks. Those two weeks were a time of healing. He played Nintendo for hours with our two sons, Jason (13) and Joshua (11). It seemed to be just what he needed. He began to get better.

He moved away from Hawaii shortly after that. He had made a connection with "The Raze". Tom Rasely had been the guitar player at church and had moved back to the mainland. The Boge followed him.

He continued to heal as he studied music with Tom. With God's help, and the help of solid friends, eventually he was able to move on with his life.

He eventually moved to New York. There he found a good wife and continued to pursue music and his relationship with the Lord. You can check out his music at www.misterfrisky.net.

One of the hardest things I ever did was to be truthful with Danny. I do not regret it. Like this verse says, I gained more favor in the end by telling the truth. To this day we are still friends.

Chapter 10

A Companion of Fools

Proverbs 13:*20 "He who walks with the wise grow wise but a companion of fools suffers harm."*

I was scared out of my mind and super-paranoid. I thought I was going to die at any moment. There I was sitting in a corner all by myself, shaking uncontrollably. My friends were all laughing and partying. "Aqualung" by Jethro Tull was blasting on the stereo. Why was everybody else so happy while I was freaking out?

I was 21 years old and my friends and I had taken some drugs. They wouldn't tell me what it was but they assured me that I'd have a good time. They did. I didn't. As it turns out, it was probably acid, better known as LSD. It affected people in different ways, and I was having a "bad trip".

How had I gotten to this place? I was raised in a good Christian home. My parents took me, or should I say, made me go to church.

I had been warned. My father used to tell me, "Birds of a feather flock together." I thought I knew better. After all, I was a know-it-all teenager. "You'll turn out like the people you hang around with," He would say. My Dad was paraphrasing Proverbs 13:20. Oh how I wish I would have heeded those words.

It started out so innocently. As teenagers, we thought we'd just drink some wine.

I remember Rule #1 I had made for myself back then: "I'll drink wine but I'll never smoke dope". Well, after a bottle of Ripple Red, Rule #2 replaced Rule #1, which was, "Well, I'll drink and smoke pot but I won't do any other drugs." After a bottle if Ripple and a few joints, Rule #2 went out the window. Rule #3 was," I'll drink wine, smoke pot and I'll take some pills." After that, came Rule #4. I thought, "Pills are O.K. but I won't stick a needle in my arm". Rule #4 was the only rule I kept. The only reason why I kept it was because I finally quit using drugs.

Now, here I was in the Navy, stationed on board a nuclear submarine. My friends and I had the day off, so we were partying at their house.

I was on active duty from 1970-71. My boat was the SSBN 654 George C. Marshall. Our sub had two crews. The crews rotated being on the boat. This was so she could be out to sea almost all the time. We had just come back from two months underwater. So we had a month of R-and-R (Rest and Relaxation).

I had become what my Dad had warned me about. I was turning out just like my friends. I was a companion of fools. I kept making rules and breaking them. When asked what they want to be when they grow up, no one ever says, “I want to be a drug addict.” But that’s where I was headed.

It happens gradually. You make small wrong decisions to please your friends. The small decisions add up to you making some big bad ones.

I made three patrols on that Sub. On every patrol one of my heroes died of an overdose. On my first patrol it was Janice Joplin. The second patrol it was Jimi Hendrix. On my third patrol, Jim Morrison, of the Doors, died. The timing of these events freaked me out.

It wasn’t long after this that I reached the end of my proverbial rope. I had a blackout. I got so wasted I couldn’t even remember what I had done the night before. I did some things I was absolutely ashamed of, things I never thought I would do.

That’s when I began to rethink my life. I needed a change but I couldn’t do it on my own. I began reading the Bible and seeking truth. I couldn’t help but marvel at the life of Jesus. He was always helping people. He healed them, fed them, taught them but most importantly, He loved them.

He loves us so much that He died an agonizing death on the cross, so that we could have a relationship with Him. Through that relationship, his presence in our lives can change us and help us to be more like Him.

I also needed to find a new set of friends. My wife and I went back to Bellevue Baptist, our old church. We made friends and got involved.

I will be forever grateful to our Pastors, Howard Engnell and Bob Brunko. Howard was my friend. He listened to all my wild ideas and he loved me. The man was a great listener. He had the patience of Job.

Pastor Bob's teaching gave me a solid foundation that has stuck with me through the years. Our church was on the south side of Chicago. It was the first integrated church with black and white people in the Baptist General Conference (now called Converge).

Many of the elders and deacons in our church were Afro-American. They loved God and loved me. I learned many of their stories of how God had helped them forgive.

One man saw his brother killed by the KKK, yet he was one of the most loving, gracious, and forgiving men I've ever met. His name was Al Sterling. Another man, Tommy Garner, frisked Pastor Howard when he came to visit his family for the first time. His wife and children had begun attending our church, but Tommy had too much fear of white people to go to church- until he met Howard.

I thank the Lord for Al Sterling, Cliff Underwood, Tommy Garner, and Jim Hicks. God used these men to mentor me from 1973-1978 until I was called to full time ministry.

My wife, Maree, and I also had a new group of friends that we began to hang out with. There was, Michael King, Dave and Susan Hamlett, Roz Steward, and Cabrina and Greely Hayes. They would come to our house after church on Sunday evenings and just hang out. The love, fellowship, and acceptance we experienced at Bellevue Baptist will always be a treasured memory. I'm sure that one day we will have quite a reunion in Heaven.

I don't know who will read this book, but let this be a warning: YOU WILL TURN OUT LIKE THE PEOPLE YOU HANG OUT WITH. Choose your friends wisely.

Chapter 11

The Lottery

Proverbs 20:21 *"An inheritance quickly gained at the beginning will not be blessed at the end."*

I remember it oh so clearly: I was at the casino playing video poker when it happened. The lights started going off on my machine with buzzers and bells sounding simultaneously. I WON! I couldn't believe it. It was too good to be true! I brought my ticket to the cashier and cashed out $240,000!

I was all smiles as I started to walk out of the casino. I had a problem though. I noticed two men following me. I didn't have to be a rocket scientist to figure out what was going on. These guys wanted my money. They were going to rob me. I started trying to figure out how I could get rid of them. I could try to fight them but they may have guns. I could try to run. No idea was foolproof. ALL OF A SUDDEN, IT CAME TO ME! I knew how I could get rid of them. I woke up!

Yes, it was only a dream. I guess I was thinking about all the lottery and casino commercials I had seen on TV. They can make winning look so glamorous. All your problems will be over. You will be able to buy whatever you want or go wherever you want. The truth is not all lottery winners end up like that.

Consider Jack Whittaker. He won $315 million in 2002. His car was robbed outside a Strip Club. They got over $500,000. He was arrested, not once, but twice for driving while under the influence. His home and office were burglarized. On top of these unfortunate events, his granddaughter died. By 2007 he had spent most of his money.

In 1990, a Florida man named Alex Toth, won $13,000,000. After his marriage fell apart he got in trouble with the IRS. He died in 2008.

According to one study, lottery winners have twice the bankruptcy rate as the general public. The problem isn't with the money. The problem is with the person. If you don't know how to handle $500 you won't know how to handle $5,000,000.

Money doesn't bring lasting happiness. Studies show that the level of happiness for lottery winners goes up at first. Then after 6 months it goes back to where it was before.

The Bible tells us in 1 Timothy 6:6-10: *"But Godliness with contentment is great gain. For, we brought nothing into this world and we can take nothing out of it. But if we have food and clothing we will be content with that.*

People who want to get rich fall into temptation and a trap and into many foolish and harmful desires that plunge men into ruin and destruction. For the love of money is a root of all kinds of evil. Some people, eager for money, have wandered from the faith and pierced themselves with many griefs."

Contentment doesn't come from money. Real contentment comes from a relationship with God, through His Son Jesus Christ. Knowing our Creator and walking with Him is worth more than all the money in the world. What good does it do to win $500,000,000 and lose your own soul? The God shaped void in all of us can't be filled with money.

The benefits of a relationship with God go beyond our comprehension.

1 Corinthians 2:9: *"However, as it is written: 'No eye has seen, no ear has heard, no mind has conceived what God has prepared for those who love Him.'"*

The writer of Proverbs asked of God to NOT to win the lottery!

Proverbs 30:8-9: *"Keep falsehood and lies far from me: give me neither poverty nor riches, but give me only my daily bread. Otherwise, I may have too much and disown you and say, 'Who is the LORD?' Or I may become poor and steal and so dishonor the name of my God."*

J. Paul Getty, who was one of the richest men in the world, once said, "I would gladly give all my millions for just one lasting marital success."

I often tell my wife, "I'm the richest guy in the whole world". She doesn't ask why. She knows what I'll say. I'll say I have the LORD, a great wife, 3 great sons, 3 wonderful daughter-in-laws, 9 awesome grandkids, a house, a car, and 3 surfboards. It doesn't get any better than that.

Chapter 12

Don't Stray from Home

Proverbs 27:8 *"Like a bird that strays from its nest is a man who strays from home."*

I was excited, scared and mad all at the same time.

"What does he look like?" I asked my Dad.

"Don't worry you'll recognize him." He answered.

I was about 12 years old. I was going to a funeral with my Dad. My Grandpa Walter was going to be there. I had never met him. I wasn't sure how to react. Should I punch him? Should I hug him? Maybe I should do both.

I never had a Grandpa growing up. My Grandpa Victor on my Mom's side died before I was born. My Grandpa Walter, on my Dad's side, left home when my Dad was a young teenager. My Dad had to drop out of High School and get a job to help support him and his Mother.

Before he left my grandmother Anna, Grandpa Walter was well known on the South Side of Chicago in the Swedish Baptist Conference. He was not only the choir director but played a mean mandolin. He played in a group called the Swedish String Band. They were quite famous. They played in churches and evangelistic outreaches all over Chicago.

My Aunt Vic, Grandma Anna's sister, kept telling her that Walter was hooking up with a young girl in the church choir. Anna wouldn't believe her. Finally, one day Anna, Aunt Vic, and my Dad all piled in the car to find out the truth. They drove from Chicago to their cottage in Sawyer, Michigan. When they got there, they found Grandpa Walter with the girl from the choir. Their world came crashing down around them, and Grandpa Walter walked out on his family. My Dad only saw his Dad more two times during his life after that. This funeral was to be one of those times.

When we arrived, I started searching the crowd for my Grandpa. Just as my Father had predicted, I instantly knew him. He had the same nose and stomach as my Dad. They were like two peas in a pod. There was no mistaking him. He was my Dad's dad. He was my Grandpa.

After my Grandma died, Grandpa Walter married that young girl from the choir. They had a daughter named Virginia. Her nickname was Ginny. My Dad knew about her but she didn't know about my Dad.

Ginny grew up to be a fine Christian woman. She married a real nice guy named Jim. They had two daughters.

Sometime after her Dad (my Grandpa Walter) died, she learned that she had a step brother- my dad.

I was there the day they met. Ginny and Jim came into our hardware store and asked for George. Dad introduced Ginny to me as his sister. They went out to lunch.

After that, they saw each other often. To say they were close would be a colossal understatement. Ginny even asked my Dad to visit her Mom in the hospital. She was dying of cancer. He went. That's the kind of man my Dad was. He read his Bible every day and he lived it.

He told my Mom, "I'll never do to you what my father did to my mom. " He kept his word. They were married for 63 years.

Ginny passed away but my Dad remained close friends with her husband Jim. Jim even remarried a close friend of my Mom and Dad's. They lived next door to them for 20 years.

I asked Uncle Jim about my Grandpa Walter once. I found out that even though my Dad only saw him twice after he left, they would talk on the phone. Uncle Jim told me that at Grandpa Walter's funeral, he overheard a friend say, "Now there was a man with a monkey on his back", meaning, there was a man who lived his life with major regrets.

When I heard that I immediately thought of Proverbs 27:8 *"Like a bird that strays from its nest is a man who strays from home."* I'm so thankful that my Dad didn't stray from home like Grandpa Walter did. May we all live our lives in such a way that on our death beds we can say, "I have no regrets!"

Chapter 13

A Cheerful Look

Proverbs 15:30a *"A cheerful look brings joy to the heart."*

No one was looking at them. Everyone was avoiding them like they had some kind of infectious disease. "These guys sure have a lot of nerve," I thought. "Just who do they think they are? Don't they realize everyone despises them? They were the ones who tried to kill my father!" I was angry and outraged to see them.

I had just gone surfing in Waikiki. I was carrying my board back to my car when I spotted them. They were Japanese Vets from World War II.

It was a special day. It was the 50th Anniversary of the unprovoked Pearl Harbor attack by the Japanese. Thousands of people lined the streets waiting for the parade, while military jets flew overhead.

These guys actually had a banner which read, "Japanese and American WW II Vets-Friends forever". I was livid. "They have no right to be here," I thought.

Memories flooded back into my mind as I thought of all the WW II Navy stories Dad told me growing up. They usually started out something like this: “Standing on the bow, shortly after midnight, seeking out the enemy, wherever he may be found.....”

One story in particular always stood out in my mind. My Dad was on an aircraft carrier in the Pacific. They were cruising along with a convoy, when all of a sudden; my Dad spotted a torpedo headed right for the carrier. He ran over to the side of the ship, stuck out his leg, and stopped the torpedo! He would roll up his pants leg and show us the scar. Then, he would get this silly grin on his face to watch our reaction. It was a well-known story in our family. My niece even got in trouble when her teacher tried to tell her it wasn’t true.

Then there were the real stories. Dad was stationed on board an LCI Landing Craft. He worked his way up to acting Chief and was in charge of the engine room.

These landing crafts were originally used to drop off soldiers or equipment on the beach. The ship sat so high out of the water that it made an easy target. Because of this, my Dad’s ship was switched from doing landings to picket duty. In other words, they were to be decoys for the Kamikaze planes.

The idea was that the inexperienced Kamikaze pilots would go after my Dad’s ship instead of one of the bigger more valuable ships, like an aircraft carrier or destroyer.

One night, for no reason, my Dad's ship and another ship were ordered to switch places in the picket line. That night a Kamikaze plane hit the engine room of the other ship. The guy standing watch in the engine room was killed. If that switch had not occurred, that guy standing watch would have been my Dad.

Another true story: My Dad was topside when the sirens went off. The Kamikaze planes had been spotted. All of a sudden one was headed for my Dad's ship, with guns blazing. My Dad was in the open, so as the plane approached; he ran, then dove and slid 20 feet behind a lifeboat. The pilot missed his ship.

Not only did I know all his stories by heart, but my Dad and I would often stay up late and watch World War II Navy movies. My Mom would protest, but Dad would just say, "It's a Navy movie." That would end the argument. Of course we would always watch "Navy Log" and "Silent Service".

As I was processing all these thoughts and memories, a still small voice said, "But I died for them too." I had learned not to argue with this Voice. It was the Holy Spirit. I needed to forgive.

I knew what I had to do. I didn't want to but I knew it was the right thing. I struggled for what seemed like hours but it was only a few seconds. As everyone was totally ignoring those Japanese Vets, I smiled and waved at them. You would have thought I had just given them a million dollars. They smiled and waved back, enthusiastically, and began speaking Japanese to me. I didn't understand a word, but in a way, I understood every word.

It was after this incident that I read an amazing true story about Captain Mitsuo Fuchida, a Japanese bomber aviator. He planned and led the attack on Pearl Harbor on December 7, 1941. He became a Christian and an evangelist after World War II. He even ministered with US Staff Sergeant Jake DeShazer.

Sergeant DeShazer was part of the Doolittle raid, the first bombing of Japan by American bombers. He spent several years as a Japanese prisoner of war where he was severely beaten, malnourished, and watched most of his flight crew die at the hands of the Japanese soldiers. While he was in prison, he remembered what he had been taught as a child and realized he needed Jesus in his life. God helped him to forgive his enemies, and in August 1945 Sergeant DeShazer was released as a POW at the end of World War II. Captain Fuchida and Sergeant DeShazer met after the war, became good friends, and ended up ministering together in Japan.

God's forgiveness, love, and power are greater than all of us. He caused two bitter enemies to forgive each other, become great friends, and even minister together. He also helped me give a cheerful look that brought joy to the hearts of five Japanese veterans.

Chapter 14

Bold as a Lion

Proverbs 28:1 *"The wicked flee when no one is pursuing but the righteous are as bold as a lion."*

"Where's Jack?" my wife Maree asked.

"Oh Maree!" my aunt Evie exclaimed.

"Where's Jack?" Ethyl, my mom demanded.

"Oh Ethyl!" my aunt gasped with even more emotion, as she paced back and forth in the room. My mom and my beautiful wife Maree were freaking out! My Aunt Evie was known for being quite dramatic, and in true Evie fashion, she was deliberately not answering their questions.

Aunt Evie had become very involved with an organization called Prison Fellowship. That evening in 1983, she had taken me to preach at I.S.P. (Indiana State Prison). It was now 10:30 p.m. on a Sunday night and I was nowhere in sight. And my dear Aunt would still not tell my wife and mother where I was.

Finally, after a few minutes of being interrogated, Evie flopped down in a chair and let the story unfold. I hadn't been taken hostage, murdered, or detained. This had been my first time inside a prison, and I felt I needed to clear my head before coming home. I had asked my aunt to drop me off so I could walk a few blocks and process what had happened that night.

Upon arriving at the prison it felt like I was in an old James Cagney movie. The walls and guard towers looked like something straight out of an old prison flick.

I.S.P. was built in the late 1800's. It is the oldest facility in the Indiana Prison system. There are ten gun towers which are manned twenty-four hours a day. It is a maximum-security facility and has housed some of the worst of the worst criminals in history.

Upon entering the prison we were searched and then escorted in. I remember getting an eerie feeling as the large, barred gates locked behind us. Fear began creeping up into my spirit like a dense fog. I began to fight the dark clouds of fear with promises from God's Word and faith began to break through like sunshine.

I wasn't afraid. I knew I had nothing to offer these men in myself. All I had to offer them was freedom in Jesus Christ. These men had done some terrible things. God still loved them. Jesus had died for them. He wanted to forgive them and set them free from the prison of their sins.

My Aunt Evie and I were escorted to the front of the prison chapel. The room was full. The worship started and those men began singing with so much exuberance that I was shocked. Here they were, convicted criminals, incarcerated in one of the most foreboding prison facilities in the Midwest, and they were singing with more joy than I had ever experienced in any church!

After the worship service ended, I was introduced. As I walked up to the pulpit the Holy Spirit fell on that place. I began to explain why I knew the Gospel was true. I talked about the martyrdom of ten of the twelve disciples, the evidence of the accuracy of the Bible, and finished up with sharing how the Lord had changed me.

I felt like I was God's channel of love and truth to these men. There was no condemnation but only the offer of salvation, free salvation, with the price paid by our loving Savior on the cross. I asked for a show of hands for anyone who would like to receive Jesus as their Lord and Savior. Almost every hand in the place went up. I prayed aloud and asked them to repeat after me. They began to pray loudly and boldly. There was no shame and no hesitation on their part. I knew God was doing something amazing.

There was an inmate in the front praying out loud. By the end of the prayer, he was literally shouting at the top of his lungs. As we all said 'Amen' he fell out into the aisle shaking. I went over to pray for him with several others. I was reminded of the Bible story in Mark 9:26." The spirit shrieked, convulsed him violently and came out."

This guy was shrieking and convulsing. I felt the still, small voice of the Holy Spirit telling me to stand up and command the evil spirit to come out of this man in the Name of Jesus. I was afraid. What if nothing happened?

I asked the inmate praying next to me, "Has this ever happened to him before?" "No, never," he replied. By this time his shaking and convulsing had increased. I was still afraid but I stood up and in a loud voice for all to hear, I said, "I command you to come out of him in the Name of Jesus!"

All of a sudden the convulsing slowed way down and stopped. Everyone was surprised but I can assure you that no one was more surprised than me. God did a great work that night. I had never felt so blessed, amazed, and humbled in my whole life.

When I got home, I recounted the events in detail to my wife and my mom. When I finished we all just sat there and let it sink in. Our righteousness as Christians is in Jesus Christ. When we walk in His righteousness we can be as bold as a lion.

I made two new friends at the prison that night that I kept in touch with for many years, Lloyd and Norman. They have both gotten out of jail since then. One of the first things they both did was to find a good church. Last I heard they were both still following the Lord. My Aunt is with the Lord now and the memory of that night will always be with me.

As Christians, we will all have challenges. At times we will all have to deal with fear, but when we decide to dwell on the righteousness we have in Christ, we can be as bold as a lion.

Chapter 15

He Will Direct Your Paths

Proverbs 3:5-6 *"Trust in the LORD with all your heart and lean not on your own understanding. In all your ways acknowledge Him and He will direct your paths."*

"That's it, Lord! I'm done."

"Go back and give it one more try."

"Lord, you know how hard I've tried already."

"Go back and give it one more try."

"Lord, this marriage isn't going to work. You know all I've been through. You know that I've gone above and beyond the call of duty. You know how hard I've tried to make this marriage work. Lord, you know that I can't go on like this any longer."

"Go back and give it one more try."

This argument went on for another hour. Like a skilled lawyer, I presented my case to the Lord. My logic was flawless. My argument was sound and there was no way I could lose. At the end of my long soliloquy, The Lord sounded a lot like a broken record. *"Go back and give it one more try."*

I have heard it said that there are 3 types of believers: believers, non-believers, and make believers. At this point in our marriage, I was a believer but I was also impulsive, immature, and very unpredictable. My wife, on the other hand, was a make believer. She wanted me to become a Christian so I would be nice. She didn't want a radical, sold out, spirit filled husband. We weren't getting along and I wanted out of my new marriage.

I wasn't the sharpest tool in the shed as far as being a Christian, but I knew the Lord's voice, and I knew He was rejecting my argument.

I told the Lord that I had a plan, and it went like this: I would take my camper van, my surfboard and move to the East Coast. I would get a minimum wage job, live in my van and surf my brains out. Great plan, right? I thought so too.

God's plan and my plan were diametrically opposed to each other. His plan was way, way, way better than anything I could ever come up with.

I did go home that night. Instead of saying goodbye to my old life and starting my new life, I said good bye to my old life and started ***God's new life.***

My wife and I made up and we had unprotected make-up sex (a great benefit of being married). 9 months later we had a son and named him Jason. Over the next few years, I kept growing closer to the Lord and seeking Him. Slowly but surely my life was beginning to radically change. I was trying so hard to be a good husband, but the closer I got to God, the more obstinate my wife became about my faith. She would even taunt me about reading my Bible!

Imagine my surprise when God called me to a ministry in Hawaii! My wife wasn't even close to being on the same page as me. I reminded God of that. I didn't hear it but I'm sure He laughed, because soon after that, my wife truly gave her heart to Jesus.

Although Maree was now following the Lord, she still wasn't ready to leave everything behind and follow me to Hawaii. I just kept praying. God slowly changed her heart and on August 28, 1978, my wife along with our two sons (Jason 5yrs. old and Joshua 3 yrs. old) boarded a United Airlines flight to Honolulu.

We went there to work with the Waikiki Beach Chaplaincy. It was a Christian evangelistic outreach in Waikiki, with Sunday morning services right on the beach. Bob Turnbull, the founder, had started out as a Youth Pastor at the Prince of Peace Lutheran Church in Waikiki. Every Sunday, from their 12th floor sanctuary, he could see thousands of tourists on the beach. Bob realized that the tourists wouldn't come to church, so he took the church to them.

Their first worship service was on the beach in front of the Hilton Hawaiian Village on Feb 8, 1969. They are still going strong today.

I worked with the Waikiki Beach Chaplaincy from 1978 to 1981. I attended Bethel College in St. Paul, MN from 1981 to 1983. After returning to Hawaii to serve in the Chaplaincy from 1983 to 1985, we planted Hope Chapel South Shore (now Hope Chapel Waikiki).

I was the senior Pastor there from 1985 to 2007. In 2007, we moved to Bridgman, Michigan and planted South Shore Fellowship. Both churches have solid pastors running them and are still ministering to their respective communities. Maree and I are now looking forward to semi-retirement, moving back to Hawaii to be near our newer grandchildren, and opportunities the Lord has for us in ministry.

Compare that last paragraph to the plan I had for my life: living in my camper van, working a minimum wage job, and surfing. I am glad I didn't lean to my own understanding. I am glad I acknowledged the Lord and went back and gave my marriage another try. I will never regret that He directed my paths, never!

"Trust in the LORD with all your heart and lean not on your own understanding, in all your ways acknowledge Him and He shall direct your paths."

Chapter 16

Servant to the Lender

Proverbs 22:7 *"The rich rule over the poor and the borrower is servant to the lender."*

There I was with my thumb out...hitchhiking. I was angry. I was screaming and swearing at all the cars that wouldn't stop and give a brother a break. The temperature was dropping and I hadn't bothered to put on my winter coat because it was only a five minute drive to the store.

Why wouldn't anyone stop?

I was in St. Paul, Minnesota. Everyone was supposed to be a Christian here, right? "What kind of Christians are you?" I shouted. "Don't you read your Bibles? I'm not a murderer or a rapist!"

Standing next to my car with my thumb out, it was quite obvious that my car had broken down. I know what you're thinking- call a tow truck! This was in 1982 and there were no cell phones.

I had been so stoked when I bought this car. It was a '72 Dodge with 4 doors and 8 cylinders. It had only cost $500, had smooth ride, and was dependable. Or at least it had been, up until this day. Our family had named the car "The Golden Eagle". That day, I renamed it "The Ruptured Duck!"

I eventually got a ride that night. Ironically, it was an atheist that picked me up and gave me a ride home!

My Dad used to paraphrase Proverbs 22:7 this way: "If you don't have it, don't spend it." It seemed as though everyone around me was running up their credit cards and borrowing money for anything and everything- new cars, clothes, houses, boats, etc.

I hadn't borrowed money to buy a vehicle since 1972. I had learned some principles concerning borrowing from God's Word and had been faithfully applying them. I was also tithing and living within my means. I was driving a used $500 car because it was what I could afford. My family and I had moved from Hawaii so that I could attend Bethel College and earn my degree in Biblical Studies. As a result, all of our extra money was going towards my college tuition.

My wife and I were both working part-time while I went to school. She was a part-time bank teller while our boys were at school. I worked nights as a janitor. It was a busy, stressful time for our family, but we just kept telling each other, "School is NOT forever!" We never had much money while I was attending school or when we were in ministry, but we always seemed to have just what we needed.

Yes, things were tight for us, financially, but God always seemed to come through for us somehow. Through the years, there were many Christmases where we didn't have any extra money for presents for our three boys. My wife and I seemed to reach a point of "no hope" every Christmas. Then, when things seemed utterly hopeless, a miracle would occur. Unexpected gifts of money would come in the mail giving us more than enough to give presents to our children.

One Christmas, after we moved back to Hawaii, our sons Jason and Joshua wanted nothing but one certain toy....a Star Wars action figure named "Yoda". Hawaii didn't always have the latest toys on the market and this particular toy was very popular. We couldn't find it anywhere. We called my sister, Annette, in Indiana and asked if she could help. She scoured the malls and found two "Yodas" and they arrived just in the nick of time!

Every Christmas we were tempted to run up our credit cards. But then we would decide to live within our means and trust God to come through. And God always came through.

One of the most amazing financial miracles we had in Hawaii happened in 1984. Housing in Hawaii is super expensive, so we had always rented. Even though we only rented, we still lived paycheck to paycheck....or as we liked to say, "From God's hand to our mouth."

We were living in a two bedroom, 900 square foot townhouse. We had just had our third child and my wife's mom had moved in with us. That meant we had 6 people living in a small two bedroom home! We began to look for a 3 bedroom townhome to rent. They were all too expensive for our budget

One day I mentioned my dilemma to a pastor friend, Mike Nelson. We were surfing Portlock Point that morning, next to the cliffs on the east side. It was my first time surfing that break. You could literally reach out and touch the cliffs as you surfed alongside them.

In between sets, I said to Mike, "My wife and I are looking to rent or buy a three bedroom townhouse." "Mine is for sale," he said. "Why don't you buy mine? My wife is a real estate agent we'll throw in her commission and give you a great price."

It seemed like a great idea until I applied for the loan. We owned a car, a motorcycle, and had $100 in savings! That was all we had! The only thing we had going for us was that we had no debt and that we were tithers.

Proverbs 3:9-10 says, *"Honor the LORD with your wealth, with the first fruits of all crops; then your barns will be filled to overflowing and your vats will brim with new wine."* My wife and I were taught by our parents that it was important to honor God with our tithes and our offerings. We had been faithfully tithing for many years. I believe God was pleased with our efforts to be obedient to Him in this area because he stepped in and blew our minds!

Several things happened simultaneously. My mother-in-law sold her home in Kentucky. My father sold his hardware store in Chicago. Both of them offered to help us with the down payment.

To our amazement we were able to BUY a three bedroom townhouse in 1986. We had a new son and had started a new church, and now lived in a new home! We were amazed, thrilled, and in awe of what God had done.

As I prayed and expressed my gratitude to God I heard him respond. "You've been faithful to me and now I am showing you that I am faithful to you."

I am so glad we were able to buy that townhouse. We sold it in 2006. It was the best investment we ever made. The only thing we had going for us is that we were tithers and we had no debt. As it turned out that was all we needed. We were free to buy because we were not "a servant to the lender."

CHAPTER 17

Don't Give Way

Psalm 25:36 *"Like a muddied spring or a polluted well is a righteous man who gives way to the wicked."*

My Dad was a little nervous as he drove us to the meeting. "I'm going to tell him we will not be open on Sundays. We may not get the store but that's just the way it is. We won't give way."

We were on our way to a meeting with a very rich and powerful man. His name was George Arquilla. After we gave our name to the receptionist we were escorted into his office by two very large Italian gentlemen. His office was huge. He wore dark glasses and spoke very softly. "Well, what do you think?" He asked. "Do you want to open a hardware store in my Heritage Plaza?"

"Yes we would," my Dad said. "But there are a few things we need first."

"What's that?"

"Well, first of all, we will not be open on Sundays."

"Are you Hollanders?"

"No sir, but Sunday is the day we go to church."

My Dad and I sat there waiting for what seemed like an eternity. This hardware store was twice as big as the one we owned currently. It was being built in the fastest growing area in the Chicago suburbs. It was a golden opportunity.

"Well," George Arquilla said. "No problem. Is there anything else?"

"Yes, there is one more thing. We need to have our $50,000 loan approved by Heritage Bank before we can sign the contract."

"That won't be a problem," he said.

"Really?"

"Really. Don't worry about it."

Later, my Dad and I found out that George Arquilla was on the board of the Heritage Bank. That loan sailed right through the approval process!

You see, that day my Dad was tempted to compromise his values. He could have said we'd stay open on Sundays but he didn't. He wouldn't compromise even if it cost him a lot of money.

That hardware store proved to be a winner. We paid off that $50,000 loan in five years!

I am not saying that George Arquilla was a wicked man; I'm just saying that George Nordgren (my Dad) was tempted to compromise his values, but he didn't. He didn't give way.

Our True Value Hardware store was closed on Sundays all the years my Dad owned it. On Sundays we went to church. That's just the way it was. We didn't give way. And my Dad never had his spring muddied or polluted because of it.

CHAPTER 18

A Gentle Answer

Psalm 15:1 *"A gentle answer turns away wrath but a harsh word stirs up hatred."*

She burst into the office in a fit of rage. "Pastor, I just don't like the way you preach. When I first came here I felt like you were preaching just to me. Now, I just don't feel anything. And also, your management skills are definitely not Biblical...."

The woman went on and on ripping the pastor up one side then down another. The pastor sat there quietly, listening intently.

When she finished, he asked her quietly, "How can I do differently?"

She sat there for about a minute and then she burst into tears. "Oh Pastor," she cried, "It's not you. My husband wants a divorce. My daughter is doing drugs and I'm totally at my wits end. Can you help me?" The pastor asked her some more questions, shared some scriptures, and prayed with her.

The pastor could have become defensive about his preaching and management skills, but he didn't. He asked what I call the Six Million Dollar Question: "How could I have done it differently?" He chose a gentle answer that turned away wrath instead of using harsh words that would have stirred up anger.

I heard this story from a pastor friend over twenty years ago. I won't mention his name...but his initials are Pastor Wayne Cordeiro of New Hope Oahu, one of the biggest Foursquare churches in Hawaii.

Years ago, a woman came to see me. She had a real problem with my preaching. I took her to task. I defended myself. I even used Scripture to really put her in her place! I really felt like I was vindicated.

I was wrong. I had forgotten all about the Six Million Dollar Question. Instead, I was drawn into continuing verbal altercations with her. As time went on, she kept finding fault with me and our fellowship.

Finally, I remembered Proverbs 15:1. I humbly asked her how I could have done things differently. As we talked the truth came out. This woman once had an abortion and could not forgive herself. Over the years, I have found that people who are hurt by someone or something in turn hurt others. They lash out because "hurt people, hurt people."

Although we came to an understanding that day, I wish I could say that after I shared some scripture that addressed her problem she got better. As far as I know she never did. She continued to go from church to church and find fault with each one.

Of all the advice and counsel I've received over the years, I would say the Six Million Dollar Question has to be one of the best. I've been married for 44 years and have been a pastor for 30. This verse and bit of advice has spared me countless hours of arguing and heartache in both my marriage and my ministry.

CHAPTER 19

Vegetables with Love

Psalm 15:17 *"Vegetables with love is better than a fattened calf with hatred."*

"Why don't you come over after class?"

"No problem."

After class, Scott drove me to his house. I had never seen such a place. There were more burglar alarms, key pads, and elevators than any place I'd ever been. This guy was rich, or at least his parents were. He lived with his parents above their furrier business on Michigan Avenue in downtown Chicago.

The place was massive. I would never have gotten in or out on my own. It was obvious these people had hundreds and thousands of dollars in furs and they took their security very seriously.

I, on the other hand, lived in a modest home with my parents and my younger sister on the far south side of the city. My Dad owned his own hardware store and we were comfortable; though far from rich.

Scott lived in luxury compared to me. He drove a Pontiac GTO- one of the first “muscle cars” ever made. We would sometimes drive through downtown Chicago like we were in the Indy 500!

At first I was envious of him. But then something happened at dinner time that changed all that. Scott, his mother, and I sat down at the table to eat some fat, juicy hamburgers, with all the fixings. As we began to eat his Dad came in, grabbed a burger, and proceeded to walk into the other room where he sat down and to eat.

I was stunned. “What just happened here?” I wondered. This was Scott’s home. This was Scott’s dad. What was going on?

So, I asked Scott why his dad was eating in the other room. “We hate each other,” he said. “We never eat together.”

Our families were so completely opposite of each other. His family was wealthy and lived together in hatred. My family was comparatively poor but we ate together and we loved each other.

It was years later when I began to read a chapter from Proverbs every day that I came across this verse. It jogged my memory and I thought of Scott and his family. This verse is true. A simple meal with love is better than a 10 course meal with hatred.

CHAPTER 20

Be Fussy

Proverbs 31:10 *"A wife of noble character who can find? She is worth more than rubies. Her husband has full confidence in her and lacks nothing of value. She brings him good, not harm, all the days of her life."*

In the early 1900's Chicago had an influx of immigrants from Sweden. One of them became a housemaid. Her name was Minnie. One day she was having problems with the kitchen faucet and had to call a plumber. He too, was from Sweden. He thought she was cute so he asked her for a date but she was fussy.

She replied, "I'll only go out with you if you go to church with me." He did. Awhile later they got married. They had five daughters. My Mom was the fourth oldest of the five. Her name was Ethyl.

Way before Ethyl was born her father had become a Christian. Every Saturday night he would gather the family together for a time of prayer. Ethyl thought that if she had a friend over to spend the night she could get out of the prayer time. A few times she even tried to tell her Dad she was sick. It made no difference. If she was sick she had to pray. If her girlfriend was visiting, she too, gathered for prayer.

All five of the Lundgren girls were raised in the Christian faith. They all married Christian men and raised their children in Christian homes. They were fussy about who they chose to marry.

In my family, we went to church every Sunday morning, Sunday evening, and Wednesday night. My Mom had a strong Christian faith that was passed on to her from her Mom and Dad. She and my Dad passed that faith on to my sisters and me.

Even though I took a detour from the way I was raised, I eventually came back. I always knew that my Mom, Dad, and Aunt Ruth were praying for me.

My wife and I began praying for our sons' wives while they were still in her womb. All three of our boys married wonderful Christian women. They were fussy.

As a pastor, I have seen many lives shipwrecked by bad marriages. Many settle for the first person that comes along. They weren't fussy.

After my parents retired they would come to visit us in Hawaii, once a year. I would always ask my Dad to give a word of encouragement to our church body when he visited. He would quote Proverbs 4:11: *"I would have you learn this one great fact, that a life of doing right is the wisest life there is."* Then he would look out over the congregation and say to the single men and women, "Be fussy." He then would go on to explain, "Wait until you find someone who loves God before you get married."

My wife and I have 9 grandchildren. I say, "Grandpa has two words for you." They have heard me say it so many times; they can say it before I can. "Be fussy."

Epilogue

Proverbs 22:1" *A good name is to be desired more than silver or gold."*

There are many people who have been a positive godly influence in my life. They all had five things in common:

1. They read their Bibles.
2. They lived their Bibles.
3. They were humble.
4. They could be corrected.
5. They were full of Jesus.

These people were not perfect by any means but they were constantly growing spiritually. They could admit when they were wrong and ask forgiveness.

There are also people in my life who have had a negative influence. They read their Bibles, BUT they didn't live them. Somehow they got off track. The traits they all had in common were:

1. They read their Bibles.
2. They didn't live their Bibles.

3. They were proud.

4. They couldn't be corrected.

5. They were full of themselves.

We all have a long way to go. We all are a work in progress. Reading and living the Word, being humble, correctable and full of Jesus are traits we should aspire to have if we are to be godly influencers on others.

Philippians 1:6 *"For I am confident of this very thing, that he who has begun a good work in you will perform it until the day of Jesus Christ."*

We need to read our Bibles asking the Lord to speak to us and change us instead of looking for scriptures to throw down on others.

I wrote down my parents' names next to Proverbs 22:1. It is my prayer that my children will one day write, "Jack & Maree Nordgren" next to this verse in their Bibles.

Other Books by the author available on Amazon:

A young Great Lakes surfer gives his life and his surfboard to Jesus. God really messes up his life and sends him to start a church in Hawaii.

Color pictures and stories of surfing on Lake Michigan

Color pictures and stories of surfing on all 5 of the Great Lakes.

How to have daily quiet time with God.

True stories of God's faithfulness by Jack's wife

To contact Jack Nordgren please email
hcbnewsletter@aol.com

About the author

Jack Nordgren grew up on the south side of Chicago. He worked for his Dad in their hardware store. He faithfully attended Bellevue Baptist Church, where at age 12, he met his future wife, Maree, at a church rolling skating party. They were married in 1970 while Jack was on active duty, serving on the USS George C. Marshall. In 1978, he and his family moved to Hawaii to work with the Waikiki Beach Chaplaincy. In 1981 they moved to St. Paul, MN where Jack attended Bethel College. He graduated with a major in Biblical Studies and a minor in New Testament Greek. In 1983 they moved back to Hawaii to work with the Waikiki Beach Chaplaincy. In 1985 they planted Hope Chapel South Shore in Waikiki (now Hope Chapel Waikiki). In 2007, they moved to Bridgman Michigan and planted South Shore Fellowship. Jack and Maree have 3 sons and 9 grandchildren.

Made in the USA
Middletown, DE
20 April 2017